Mosquitoes

Mosquitoes

Mary Ann McDonald

THE CHILD'S WORLD®, INC.

Library of Congress Cataloging-in-Publication Data
McDonald, Mary Ann.
Mosquitoes / by Mary Ann McDonald.
p.   cm.
Includes index.
Summary: Examines the physical characteristics,
behavior, habitat, and life cycle of mosquitoes.
ISBN 1-56766-635-3 (lib. bdg. : alk. paper)
1. Mosquitoes—Juvenile literature.
[1. Mosquitoes.]   I. Title.
QL536.M33   1999
595.77'2—dc21   98-49135
CIP
AC

Photo Credits

ANIMALS ANIMALS © Donald Specker: 16
© Bill Beatty/Wild & Natural: 26
© Dwight R. Kuhn: cover, 2, 13, 15, 24
© D. Yeske/Visuals Unlimited: 19
© 1999 E.R. Degginger/Dembinsky Photo Assoc. Inc.: 10
© Fred Whitehead/Colephoto: 23
© Jack Glisson/Kentucky Up Close: 29
© John Eastcott/Yva Momatiuk/The Image Works: 6
© Meckes/Ottawa, The National Audubon Society Collection/Photo Researchers: 30
© William E. Ferguson: 9, 20

On the cover...

Front cover: This female mosquito is sucking blood from the photographer's hand.
Page 2: This male mosquito is resting on a flower.

Table of Contents

Chapter	Page
Meet the Mosquito!	7
Where Do Mosquitoes Live?	8
What Do Mosquitoes Look Like?	11
Why Do Mosquitoes Buzz?	12
What Do Mosquitoes Eat?	14
How Do Mosquitoes Drink Blood?	17
Where Do Mosquitoes Lay Their Eggs?	21
How Do Mosquitoes Live Through Winter?	25
Do Mosquitoes Have Enemies?	27
Are Mosquitoes Pests?	28
How Can We Control Mosquitoes?	31
Glossary, Index, & Web Sites	32

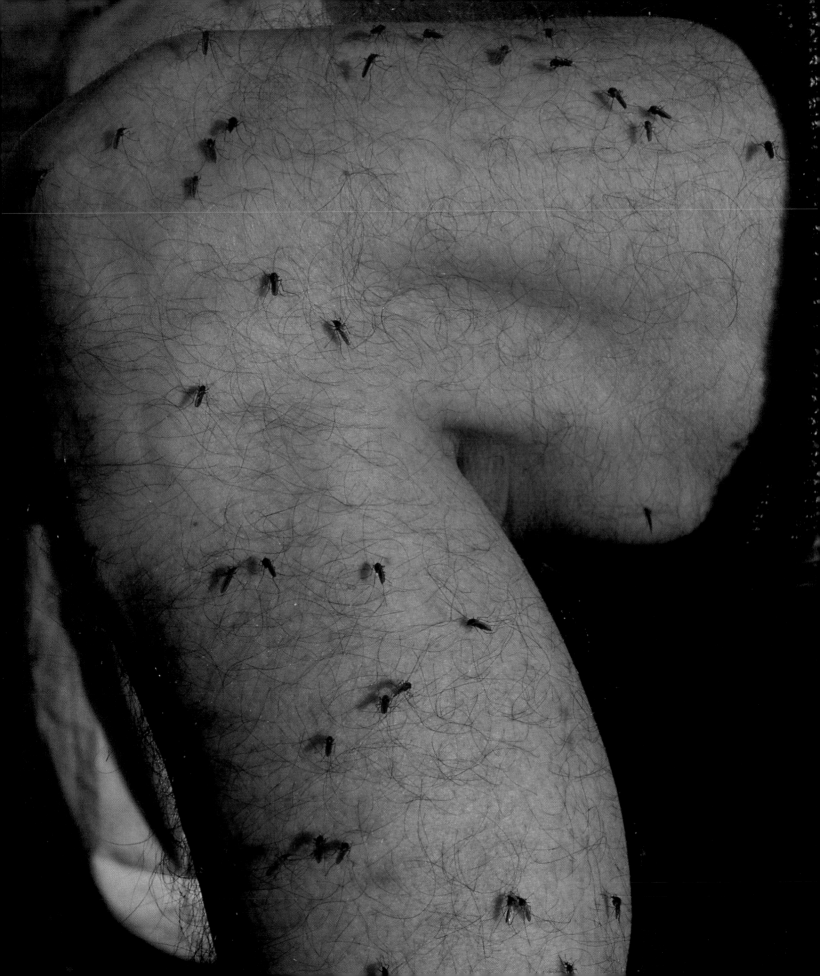

It's a hot, hazy day in the middle of summer. You're sitting at your favorite fishing hole waiting for something to take your bait. Suddenly, you notice a small bug as it lands on your arm. As you watch, it pushes its long snout into your skin. After a short time, the bug flies away, and your skin itches a little. What was this creature? It was a mosquito!

← These mosquitoes are drinking blood from someone's leg.

Where Do Mosquitoes Live?

Mosquitoes live almost everywhere in the world. They can be found in steamy jungles, city parks, and even in the cold north. Mosquitoes like areas near water. They also like places that are shady and dark. Thick forests or areas such as swamps are favorite places for mosquitoes.

This mosquito is resting on a leaf. ⇒

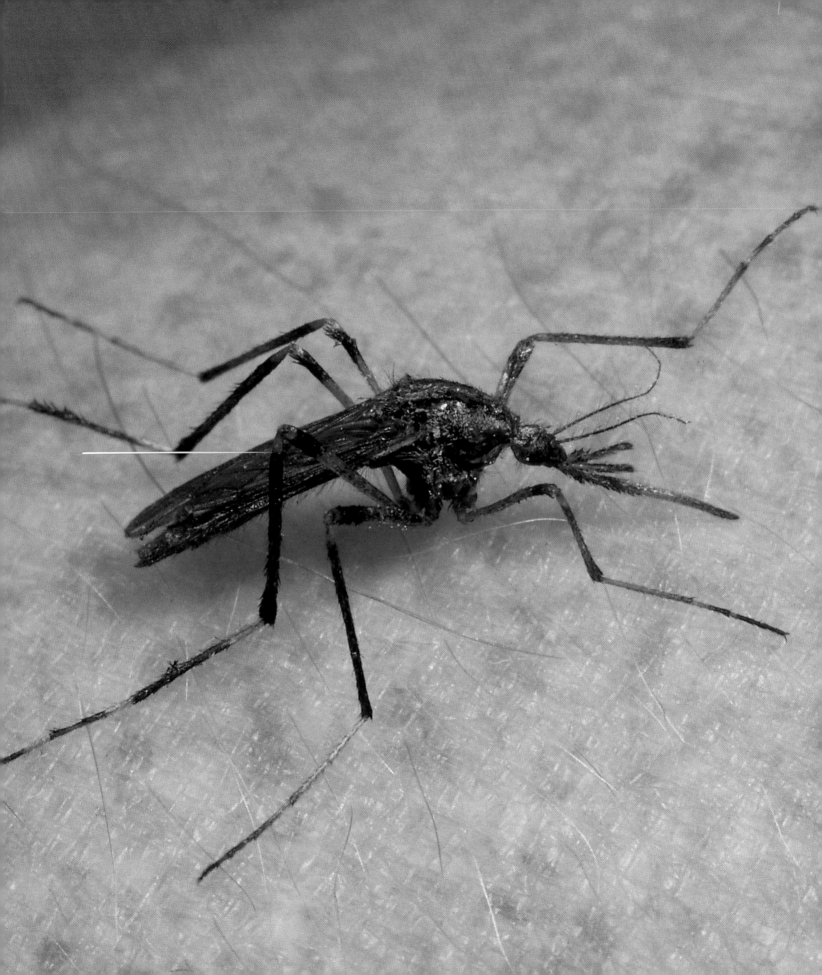

What Do Mosquitoes Look Like?

Mosquitoes are **insects.** Insects are animals that have three different body parts: the head, the **thorax,** and the **abdomen.** The thorax is the insect's chest area. The abdomen is its belly. Most insects also have two sets of wings on their backs. Mosquitoes' wings are long and narrow.

Mosquitoes have long, thin legs with scales on them. They also have two feelers on their heads called **antennae.** All mosquitoes have a long, skinny beak, too. This beak is called a **proboscis** (pro–BAH–sis).

⇐ It's easy to see this mosquito's body parts as it sits on a person's arm.

Why Do Mosquitoes Buzz?

Most people hear mosquitoes before they see them. That's because mosquitoes make a high whining or buzzing sound as they fly. The sound is caused by the fast movements of the mosquito's wings. When the wings move up and down, the scales on the mosquito's body move back and forth. Female mosquitoes make a very high noise when they fly. Male mosquitoes are harder to hear.

This female has just finished feeding and is flying away. ⇒

What Do Mosquitoes Eat?

Male and female adult mosquitoes eat different things. Males feed mostly on a sweet liquid called **nectar** that plants make. They also eat fruit. Female mosquitoes eat something very different—blood! Female mosquitoes will eat the blood of almost any animal, including people. Blood helps the eggs that are inside the female to grow and develop the right way.

This male mosquito is feeding on a piece of fruit. ⇒

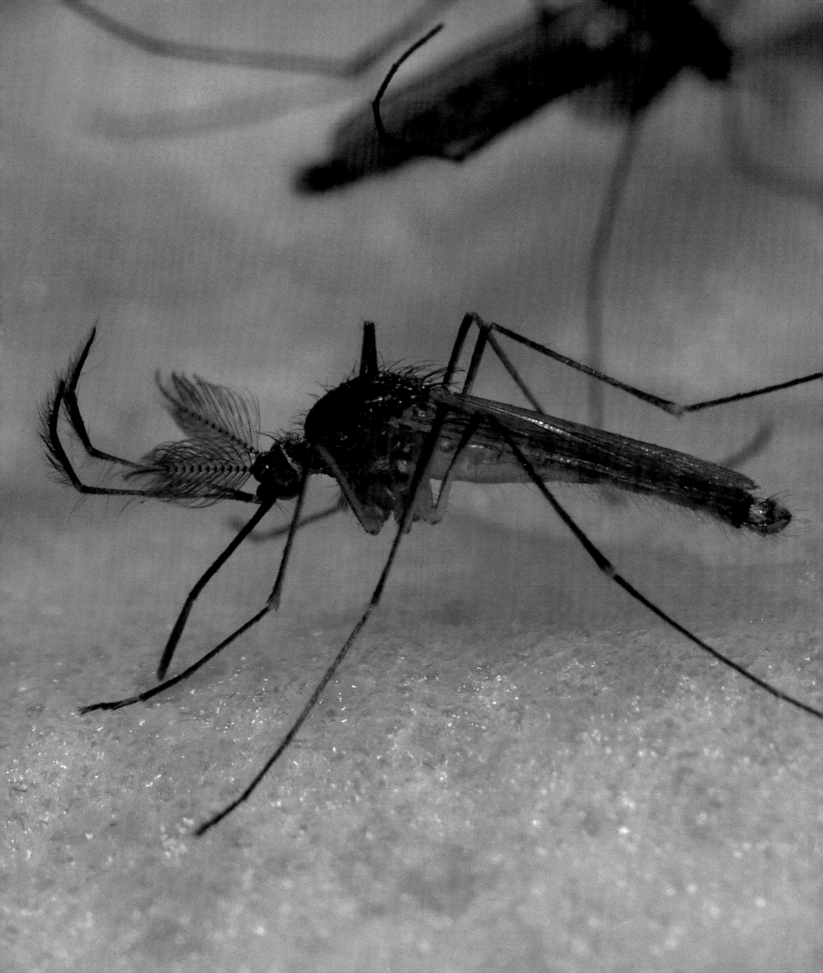

How Do Mosquitoes Drink Blood?

When she is hungry, a female mosquito flies around until she finds an animal on which she can land. When she finds a soft spot on the animal's skin, the mosquito pokes a hole with her long proboscis. She then pushes a special juice called **saliva** from her body into the animal's skin. Her saliva makes the blood easier for her to suck up.

⇐ You can see the blood in this female's belly as she feeds.

When she is finished, the mosquito simply flies away. A little while later, a bump starts to form over the hole the mosquito made. The animal's body does not like the mosquito's saliva inside it. As it heals, the bump becomes red and itches a lot. We call these bumps *mosquito bites.*

This girl has an itchy mosquito bite behind her ear. ⇒

Where Do Mosquitoes Lay Their Eggs?

Most females lay their eggs near water. They might lay them near lakes or ponds, or even in old tires filled with rainwater! Others lay their eggs in dirt, snow, or ice. Some kinds of mosquitoes lay their eggs one by one. Others lay them in huge clumps called *rafts*. These clumps float in the water until the eggs hatch.

⟸ This mosquito egg raft is floating in a pond.

After about two days, the eggs hatch and small **larvae** push their way out. Instead of looking like adult mosquitoes, the larvae look like tiny worms. As they grow, the larvae feed on tiny plants and animals they find in the water. To breathe, mosquito larvae have a special tube at the end of their body. They float near the surface of the water and breathe air just as you do.

These mosquito larvae are floating just under the surface of a pond. ⇒

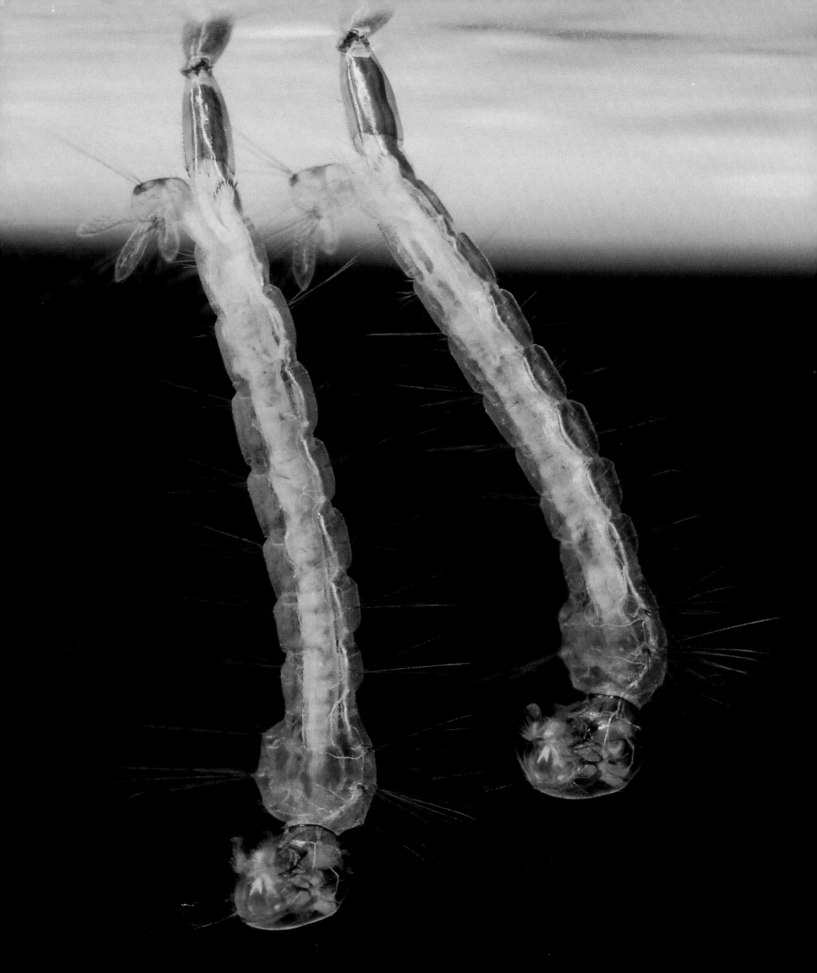

How Do Mosquitoes Live Through Winter?

Adult mosquitoes need warmer weather to live. When cold weather comes, the adults die. The eggs and larvae, however, can stay alive during the cold winter months. They just stop growing and wait for warmer weather. When spring comes, the eggs and larvae slowly warm up. When the time is right, the eggs hatch and the larvae start growing again.

⇐ This adult mosquito is resting on top of some rainwater.

Do Mosquitoes Have Enemies?

Mosquitoes have lots of enemies. They are a favorite food for birds, bats, snails, and spiders. They are even eaten by other insects! A brown bat can eat 1,000 mosquitoes every night. Fish eat thousands of mosquito eggs and larvae, too. And people are always ready to swat pesky mosquitoes that bite them.

⇐ This *damselfly* has caught a mosquito for dinner.

Are Mosquitoes Pests?

Most mosquitoes simply cause people to itch and scratch. Some types, though, can make people very sick. In some parts of the world, sicknesses such as *malaria* and *yellow fever* are spread by mosquitoes.

One way to keep mosquitoes from biting you is to use a bug spray. Wear long sleeves and pants in places where there are lots of mosquitoes, too. If mosquitoes can't find your skin, they won't be able to bite.

This girl is using a spray to keep mosquitoes away. ⇒

How Can We Control Mosquitoes?

The easiest way to control mosquitoes in your yard is to get rid of places where water stands still. Drain any cans, old tires, and toys that have filled up with rainwater. Then the mosquitoes will have no place to lay their eggs.

You can also use the animals that eat mosquitoes to keep these pests away. Building bat and birdhouses in your yard gives these animals a nice place to live. Then they will start to eat the mosquitoes that would otherwise bother you!

Glossary

abdomen (AB–doh–men)
An abdomen is the stomach part of an insect.

antennae (an-TEN-nee)
Antennae are long feelers on an insect's head. Mosquitoes use their antennae to explore the world around them.

insects (IN–sekts)
Insects are small animals that have three body parts and six legs. Mosquitoes are insects.

larvae (LAR–vee)
Most young insects are called larvae. Mosquito larvae look like tiny worms.

nectar (NEK-ter)
Nectar is a sweet liquid that forms in plants. Male mosquitoes drink plant nectar.

proboscis (pro–BAH–sis)
A proboscis is a mosquito's beak. Mosquitoes have a very long proboscis that they use for feeding.

saliva (suh–LY–vuh)
Saliva is a juice that many animals have in their mouths. A mosquito's saliva makes blood easier to suck up.

thorax (THOR–ax)
A thorax is the chest part of an insect's body.

Web Sites

Learn more about mosquitoes:

http://www.lanakids.com/mosquito.html

http://www-rci.rutgers.edu/~insects/mosbiol.htm

Learn how to keep mosquitoes from biting you: http://www.mosquitoes.com

Index

abdomen, 11

antennae, 11

appearance, 11

biting, 7

drinking blood, 14, 17

eggs, 14, 21, 22, 25, 31

enemies, 27, 31

flying, 12, 18

food, 14

larvae, 22, 25

legs, 11

location, 8

malaria, 28

mosquito bite, 18

mosquitoes as pests, 28

proboscis, 11, 17

protection from, 28, 31

rafts, 21

saliva, 17, 18

scales, 11, 12

sounds, 12

thorax, 11

wings, 11, 12

yellow fever, 28

young, 14, 21, 22

winter, 25